GROWING TRAP

A Reliable Plan to Avoid Life's Traps and Improve Yourself

By

Gregory A. Johnston

Contents

Introduction

We can develop quickly as children. Every year, we get larger, become more capable, move up through the grades, and take in all around us. But only to a certain extent does this happen "naturally." Growth no longer comes as effortlessly by the time we start our first full-time work or graduate from college. We must take initiative if we want to keep getting better and moving forward in life. The growth trap, as I like to call it, occurs when one does not actively work toward improving oneself and subsequently finds oneself in a life-stuck state.

In each stage of your life, you have the potential to get caught in a growth trap. The growth trap is like pulling a boulder up a hill: you have to work constantly to keep the rock from tumbling. It doesn't matter if you want to develop physically, emotionally, financially, or mentally—you need to put forth the effort every day to keep getting better. Otherwise, you will tumble into a growth trap like a boulder on a slope. Being proactive is a part of growing.

Chapter 1

How to Be Intentional About Your Growth

We're still talking about growth because it makes sense that we should all continue to develop. Do you have a strategy for advancing your career or business? You must make an effort to grow; it won't just happen.

What makes you valuable, exactly?

Do you have a strategy for improving yourself? to manage a better company?

Anything that you want to grow needs your assistance; this assistance may take the form of creating the ideal climate,

giving it the proper nutrition, or shielding it from hazardous elements.

Growing purposefully entails making plans and carrying them out rather than sitting about waiting for something to happen to spur you into action. What steps will help your company, service, or relationship?

Getting results does not necessarily imply growth. You simply have a talent for hitting targets. However, reaching our goals is a by-product of growth.

James Allen stated that "people are eager to better their surroundings but are unwilling to improve themselves" in his book "As A Man Thinketh So Is He." As a result, they are still bound.

When a challenge arises, view it as an opportunity to increase your capacity.

When you become intentional about your growth, you will be able to overcome it. Each challenge and obstruction is an opportunity for improvement, growth, and accumulation.

Between where you are and where you aspire to go, there is a gap, which John Maxwell refers to as "the growth gap." He claims that the majority of individuals are unaware of how simple it is to make gaps that prevent them from developing and reaching their full potential.

The law of intentionality applies in this situation; you must be purposeful and intentional in all of your actions to achieve your goals.

Here are 8 growth myths that may be preventing you from starting deliberate growth, along with solutions.

1. The Assumption Gap – This is assuming that you will automatically develop because we assume that we will develop and improve as you grow from children to adults. Life, however, does not operate that way.
The same is true for your company; expansion won't just happen.

- **You must be intentional and aware of your intentionality if you want to stay at the top of your game. No one, nor any company, ever advances by chance. Own your accountability for it.**

2. The Knowledge Gap - When you lack the knowledge necessary to advance. Most individuals always opt for the difficult route when learning new things; they attempt something without any prior knowledge, fail, and then look for information later.

- **Get the information by taking the course, hiring the coach or mentor, and purchasing the item. Close the knowledge gap between what you** know—about 2%—and what you don't know—a startling 98 percent.

3. The Timing Gap - When should we start, since now isn't the right moment? Do you know about the decreasing intent law?

According to this, the likelihood that you won't complete an action you should take right away increases the longer you delay. Be aware that deciding to do something is not the same as actually doing it. Right or wrong, we simply don't respond to situations as swiftly as we should.

- **DO IT NOW.** There is no better time to take that action. Make that call. Send that message. Just do it. Capture it. Assign it. Act on it.

4. The Fear of Making a Mistake Gap.

To grow intentionally, one must venture into the unknown; this may entail not having all the answers, which can be

frightening and result in failure or humiliation anxiety. Making mistakes is a necessary part of growth, and I adore the proverb that states, "If you're not making mistakes, you're not maximizing your potential."

- Get over your fear; making mistakes is a terrific sign that you are progressing.

5. The Perfection Gap - "I have to have everything perfect before I begin." The result will be procrastination.

- You can only achieve progress by moving forward; there is no other way to perfect something.

6. "I don't feel like doing it," The Inspiration Gap

Do you realize how deceitful your emotions maybe?

You'll be stuck in the realm of inertia if you wait for other people to motivate you.

- Yes, it's that easy. You just have to train yourself to push past your emotions and carry on regardless of how you feel. Don't hesitate to act, even in business.

7. "Others are better than I am" - The Comparison Gap

Have you ever entered a room with other brilliant people and felt intimidated? I

have, but I've since discovered that it's a great learning opportunity.

- You lose out if you withdraw and avoid those situations; instead of comparing yourself to others, take advantage of the chance to absorb knowledge from outstanding individuals.

8. The Expectation Gap: "I thought it would be easier than this" What notable achievement has been accomplished without much difficulty? Your company's success won't come easily because deliberate growth begins with preparation, which takes time. No overnight success has ever happened without years of planning.

- The sooner you decide to intentionally pursue your growth, the clearer things will become, the more doors will open, and the faster things will go.

- To Change That

- Make the proper inquiries

Which destination do you seek? How far do you think this company will progress? What path do you want to take?

Empower yourself to become the promising version of yourself. This will trickle down to your staff, clients, and other aspects of your business.

- Act right away.

Nike was correct. Simply complete it right away and with urgency. Do it even if it's unfamiliar; don't erect your barriers.

- **Face your phobias**

Everyone experiences some level of fear, regardless of who they are, but we must confront this fear with faith. Develop faith and choke off fear.

- **From unintentional to intentional progress,**

The outcomes make it simple to distinguish between accidental and deliberate growth. Avoid becoming stuck in a rut because it will prevent you from achieving your goals.

Determine what you want, then assess your progress every day

to determine if you're getting there. Both the decisions you make and the ones you don't are under your control. You can either plan for development learning before you make a mistake or you can either hope for growth or be unintentional in the process of learning from your mistakes. Consider yourself a victim or consider yourself a student and seek.

The future of your life and business depends on the decision you make! You have to take the initiative if you want to grow. Check out my podcast on deliberate growth to learn more.

Chapter 2

Stagnation in Your Mental Health and Wellbeing

Growth is proof of life. There are times when we thrive and shine in life. We have so much enthusiasm to achieve our goals and perhaps exceed them. Then there are times when we don't feel up to the task - times, when it appears like every part of life, has come to a halt and some unseen force is preventing us from moving forward.

It could manifest in your life as a sense of immobility or a lack of closeness and growth in your relationship. Nothing can ever thrill you enough to take action. You're trapped in a never-ending cycle of monotonous everyday chores, accompanied by a paralyzing fear of being locked in a rut.

Simply speaking, stagnation is a lack of progress and development. Even in the absence of a comprehensive scale for evaluating stagnation, there are warning signals to look for, such as:

- Goals that have been put off for too long
- lack of motivation to achieve anything

- For comfort, people turn to sleep, entertainment, and other thoughtless activities.
- Having that impression that you are not living up to your full potential

Stagnation in your life is frequently a symptom of underlying concerns.

- Taking care of such concerns will help you get back on track. It won't happen immediately, but you can get out of a rut one step at a time.

The Effects of Stagnation on Mental Health

It can be challenging to see others improve while you appear to be trapped in the same position. Such circumstances make you mistrust your ability to affect change in your life. At this point, there is a propensity to rely on external sources to drive change. You become frustrated and upset when these external things fail or disappoint you because you have no control over them.

Stuck people are more likely to fall into depression. Depression is exacerbated by low self-esteem or self-criticism. Feeling that you have no clear path forward in your relationships, friendships, work, or self-development can be detrimental to your self-esteem. You know it makes you sad, yet there seems to be no other option.

How to Proceed

To get out of a rut, you must adopt the mindset of making things happen rather than waiting for the situation to improve on its own. To make your relationship work, talk to a therapist or enroll in couples counseling. It entails discussing your motivation concerns with your pals and holding each other accountable.

Being paralyzed by fear might cause you to become immobile. Setting and desiring particular goals isn't always a difficulty. The true issue is a fear of failure that prevents you from doing. Overthinking the amount of work involved and the risk of blunders prevents you from realizing that being open to mistakes is what allows you to progress. It is advantageous to divide your tasks into little segments. In this manner, with each try, you can go one step closer to your goal.

You may be the only one who is still standing while the rest of the world is moving, but this is not the case. Many people from many areas of life are in the same situation. According to a recent study, 69 percent of Americans feel stuck in the same old pattern.

Recognizing that you are not alone in your situation makes it easier to live with this transient state. Accepting the circumstance for what it allows you to concentrate on positive steps that will get you moving. You may need to break some old habits to make room for a new way of doing things.

At the end of the day, acknowledging that the ball is in your court and that you are the only one who can take the necessary actions to get out of a rut is the first step toward productivity. The happiness and contentment you seek in your life come from within, not from elsewhere.

Ways to Break Free From Life Stagnation

There are times when we grow and thrive on our journey of development. We are always driven and psyched up, determined to achieve our objectives.

Then there are moments when we become stuck. We are demotivated and uninspired. We keep putting off making plans. We frequently break out of one rut only to fall back into another.

How can you know if you're stuck? Here are some warning signs:

If you've been procrastinating on your goals for a long time,
If you never have the desire to achieve anything,

- If you continue to seek solace through sleep, eating, games, mindless activities, and entertainment,
- If you know you should do something but keep putting it off,
- If you haven't accomplished anything new or substantial in the last month, two months, or three months,

- If you have a strong feeling that you are not living up to your full potential,
- When we experience stagnation in our lives, it is a sign of deeper concerns.
- Life stagnation, like procrastination, is a symptom of a problem. It's simple to beat ourselves up about it, but this isn't going to help.

Here are five methods to help you break free from this rut. They will not suddenly transform your life in one night (such improvements are never permanent because the foundations are not created), but they will assist you in regaining momentum and getting back on track.

1. Recognize You're Not Alone, First

Everybody experiences a period of stagnation. In addition to not being alone, this is also common. It's astounding how many of my customers genuinely deal with the identical situation, even though they all come from various walks of life, have varying ages, and have never met.

It will be much easier to go through this time if you realize you are not alone in this. You are only fighting yourself when you attempt to "fight it." Tell yourself it's okay, acknowledge this situation, and accept it. You can then concentrate on taking the beneficial actions that will benefit you.

2. Find Your Source of Inspiration Stability results from the absence of anything that motivates you to act. It's understandable if you are suffering stagnation if you don't make it a habit to create goals and instead just let daily responsibilities take care of yourself.

Without limitation what would you do? What would you desire if you could have anything you wanted? The answers to

these queries will serve as your onward momentum.

However, even if you have expertise in setting objectives, there are moments when those goals no longer seem worthwhile. It happens to me too, and it's common. Since our emotional states have changed since we initially set our goals, we occasionally lose sight of them. At times, our priorities shift, and we decide we no longer wish to work for those objectives. However, we are unaware of this, and as a result, we put off doing our tasks until they become a significant issue.

If it applies to you, it's time to revisit your objectives. Pursuing objectives that no longer inspire you is pointless. Discard your previous objectives (or simply set them aside) and consider your current priorities. So go after them.

3. Take a Break for Yourself

When was the last time you gave yourself a genuine break? 30 days? six months 1 year? Never? Perhaps it's time for a break. Someone who works for a long time may lose sight of who they are and what they want, which can lead to disillusionment.

Go take a few weeks off from work. At the very least, a few days; ideally, a few weeks or months. Some of my former coworkers resigned from their employment and took time off to reflect on their lives. Of course, some of us may not have that luxury, in which case we can limit our absence to a few weeks.

Get away from your job and your daily routine by traveling somewhere else. Take advantage of the opportunity to gain a fresh outlook on life. Consider your life's purpose, your desires, and the future you see for yourself.

These are significant issues that demand careful consideration. It is more important to start looking for the answers than it is to find them all at once.

4. Change Up Your Habits

Being in the same setting, performing the same actions repeatedly, and running into the same people might make us stale. This is particularly true if the people you spend the most time with themselves are unchanging.

Rearrange the situation. Start small by switching up your morning routine, such as taking a different route to work. Have lunch with various coworkers who you haven't had much interaction with. If there are free and convenient seats at your job, work in a different cubicle. On weekends and throughout the weekday evenings, take a different course of action. Develop several routines, such as daily exercise, listening to a new podcast while driving to work, reading a book, etc. (Here Are 6 Proven Ways To Make New Habits Stick). The various contexts will provide you with various stimuli, which will cause you to have various ideas and take various actions.

I can usually tell when I'm stagnating because of what's causing it. Sometimes it's the setting I'm in, other times it's the company I've been keeping, and still other times it's my way of life. The majority of the time, it's a mix of all of these. I can get myself out of the rut by switching things up.

5. Take Small Steps at First

Another cause of stagnation is being paralyzed by dread. Perhaps you truly want to achieve this specific objective, but you aren't moving forward. Are you unable to handle the amount of labor

required? Are you concerned that you will err? Is your need for perfection controlling you and making you paralyzed?

Stop insisting that it must be flawless. Such a view is harmful, not beneficial. Being willing to make mistakes and learn from them is exactly how you advance.

Break the task at hand down into tiny, little steps, and then proceed one tiny step at a time. Due to his fear of failing, one of my clients had been inactive for a while. He didn't want to act in a way that would lead to another error. He has, however, done nothing for two to three years since he doesn't want to make a mistake.

On the other hand, even if you only take a single action, you will have advanced, error or not. Even if you appear to make an "error," you receive feedback to proceed with caution in the future. If you hadn't taken action, you would have never known that.

Chapter 3

Breaking Habits: Resilience in the Face of Failure

Why Creating Great Habits Requires Planning for Failure.

"I certainly comprehend allowing for certain failures, but it appears that this is the most challenging aspect. How do you stop one failure from leading to two, then three, and before you know it, months have passed and you are still unaware that you have abandoned the goal?

Begin modestly. Start with a few quick victories, then gradually gain momentum.

Take a long view. Consider your end goals and keep in mind why you started a habit or set a goal.

Do not fear failure. Teak breaks are OK if they increase the sustainability of your progress.

Rob's query regarding preventing one failure from leading to other failures is one that I can relate to. I've experienced slipping a little bit and then sliding much further. I had chicken fingers for lunch, then somehow manage to use that as an excuse to have a cheesesteak for dinner. For one or two days, I don't go to the gym, and then I occupy that time with something else. The list continues.

Like Mark, many people use the "break the chain" strategy or other methods to add activities to their calendars to stay on task. Numerous psychological studies have shown that, even though such tactics don't support your behaviors, they can nonetheless influence your brain to keep them. Instead of mending the faulty system, I do not want to just add additional processes to it, like placing a bandage on a severed arm or filling a leaking bucket with water. Instead, I work to identify and fix any problems with the system as a whole. Here's how to do that in three steps:

1. Take lessons from the encounter

What happened? Why?

If you let it, failure can be a very upsetting experience. If you take the time to learn from failure, it can help you become stronger.

Spend some time analyzing what went wrong and why after a failure. Following your realization of the situation's truth, you should take the following two actions:

2. Controlling expectations

Was the goal achievable? Or were you just putting yourself in a bad situation?

Failure is the difference between what you intended to do and what you accomplish. Dissatisfaction is the controversy between intentions and existence.

The long-term drive is not going to be helped by consistently failing and facing disappointment. Your self-confidence is damaged, which causes self-doubt. You have two choices on how to deal with that. The first step is to raise your accomplishments. To encourage more reasonable expectations is the second. I advise beginning with that method because it is the most long-term option and can help you get better results.

Decide what you can accomplish. Sometimes I don't even quantify my objectives. For instance, I make an effort to help someone every day. It could be as substantial as giving money or your time, but most of the time it's just as simple as telling someone you love them or writing an article like this. You're less likely to suffer the letdown of unmet expectations and more likely to experience the inspiring dopamine rush of success when your expectations are more reasonable.

3. Make the end goals a motivator.

Was the objective in line with your ends and objectives?

Goals are great, but I much prefer systems, as I've stated in past writings. A goal is something particular and quantifiable that you hope to accomplish by a certain date. A system is a routine that you follow to get results and improve over time. Even though I like systems more, I still make goals— just not for the same reasons or in the same way that other people do. I don't use the term "S.M.A.R.T." objectives or anything similar. I created "end goals." The final results that you hope to accomplish are known as end objectives. They stand for your beliefs, as well as what gives you joy and fulfillment. Ultimate goals are distinct from "means"

because goals are the results we believe are necessary to achieve our end goals. Among the means, ambitions are aspirations to become a doctor or earn a million dollars, etc.

Chapter 4

Are You Trying to Force Growth

The notion that you can force or demand growth as a leader is flawed and limiting. Although it may appear to be a tough and powerful presence, it hides a leader who is either losing control or is hesitant to hand control over to anyone else.

Leaders who view the workplace and the people working there as an object that can be tugged, pushed, and beaten into the desired results that it wants to reach—almost forcing it at gunpoint to achieve the aims that have been put out before them—are a common sight in the workplace. The firm is aware of what it wants, but it is oblivious to what is necessary to attain that end successfully, efficiently, and with a long-term favorable outcome because it is driven by the desire to have it sooner rather than later.

When goals and financial outcomes are being met, forced growth leadership is frequently hidden, but it usually pops up at the beginning of the fiscal year when new budgets and goals are announced for the company and its employees. Leaders that have a forced attitude will present this information without a strategy and with no further information other than the precise statistics needed by the company to meet a goal.

When the goals or results are not met, this style of leadership is more obvious.

The leader's demands get more adamant as the pressure increases. Targeted individuals may be questioned about their performance and results as though they were the cause of the company's overall poor performance.

How do you recognize a forced growth mentality?

As the pressure starts to build, there are obvious signals that become obvious if the company is being run with this approach. These consist of;

Blame

Blame Leadership focuses on departments or persons that are forming to identify the root cause. Increased micromanagement, increased targeting of individuals, and more layoffs are all to be expected.

Inconsistent

An action plan is implemented only to be abandoned in favor of a different strategy a few days or weeks later when the leadership appears to be continually changing their mind. There is a conflict in the requirements that makes the job environment complicated.

Tension

The atmosphere at work gets heated, hostility and fury seem to be growing, and stress levels within the company will rise. To avoid getting caught in the crossfire, people will make every effort to avoid one another and the leadership. As their irritation increases, people will start to get angry over smaller things.

Communication Issues

The workplace only understands that "Money" is what the company wants. People start to tune out what is said and expressed due to the environment that has been created and the bad emotional state. An environment of "White Noise," or meaningless static and humming, will have been produced as a result of resentment and avoidance.

Employee Retention

There is a serious problem with your company when customers start to quit of their own volition. This is the last expression of disapproval for the administration. Because there is a lack of respect, trust, and confidence in the environment, progress will never be made.

What should I do next?

It is your responsibility as a leader to set up the company such that everyone is working together during both good and bad times. I'm not only referring to your company as a whole; I'm also referring to the people that work there. The aforementioned climate results in forced expansion rather than leadership-driven growth.

Similar to trying to force a tree to grow, a firm cannot be forced to expand. If you have not prepared the ground, provided it with the environment to grow, and understood it for what it is, then it will die. You can yell at it, keep trimming it back, pull on it, hang off of it, and tell it what it needs to achieve all you want. In the end, you can provide it with more of what it requires but never more of what you desire.

How can the environment be altered?

When the environment is harmed, you have to make investments to create a new one. Yes, spending money may be necessary when you need more money, but if you keep moving in the same direction, the only other alternative is having no money.

Key adjustments are necessary for:

- Put your ego aside and pay attention to people around you.
- You don't have all the solutions, so quit believing you do; try some of the ideas that other people have.
- Before deciding to shift course, commit to a plan and give it and the people a chance to implement it and make it work.
- Be brave enough to own your mistakes.
- Find out what the people in your company "need" to advance and prosper over the long term, not just now.
- Stop attempting to control everything and give employees more room to perform their duties.
- Before you consider firing someone, take a look at what is

preventing them from performing their tasks successfully and fix it.

As a leader and a businessperson, you cannot be the drowning person who drags everyone else under to try and save yourself, sacrificing people who would be willing to help you if you would just pause and pay attention.
The emotional state of employees who work for your company ultimately determines how well they perform; alter this, and your company will change.

Chapter 5

How to maintain your course

It's not enough to just set goals. See what it takes to bring your ideas to fruition.

You understand the importance of setting objectives and developing a long-term plan for your work and personal life. You now know how to set and achieve goals. Nevertheless, do you have a technique for fulfilling your purposes and staying committed to your plan over time?

The following advice will help you to better adhere to your plans.

It's time to record it. Make a written record of your career goals so you don't forget them and can keep tabs on how far you've come. With a plan that is clear, precise, feasible, practical, and time-bound you are more likely to follow through (SMART). The refrigerator door or the mirror in your bedroom are good places to keep a copy of your plan handy.

Decide on a timetable and stick to it. Set one of two short-term objectives that you can accomplish in the next few days or weeks. After that, set more short-term objectives that can be accomplished in a few months. Your long-term goals will become increasingly apparent as you progress through your to-do list.

You deserve a reward. You will have to put in a lot of effort to reach your goals. When you complete a task, whether large or small, treat yourself to a modest reward. These incentives will keep you going.

Make sure you have an accountability buddy. You mustn't strive to accomplish your goals by yourself. Set up a support network of people who will keep you on track. Someone you know, someone you're working with, or even your supervisor can serve as a sounding board (or corrections agent). Timelines and encouragement are two things your partner will be there for when you're facing setbacks.

There is no such thing as "too old" to outline a new objective or vision.

www.ingramcontent.com/pod-product-compliance
Lightning Source LLC
Chambersburg PA
CBHW070608160726
48003CB00005B/2158